W9-DAO-966

Date _____

This book is a gift

to _____

from _____

with best wishes

for a lifetime of

good days and special times.

THANK YOU FOR BUYING THIS VERY SPECIAL BOOK.

This book is the first in a series of special projects and programs commemorating the 20th anniversary of the founding of Camp Good Days & Special Times.

It is our 20th anniversary gift to children everywhere. The proceeds will benefit Camp Good Days now and help support children's oncology camps throughout the United States and Canada in the future.

By buying the book to share with the children in your life, you are helping to bring the joy of summer camp to boys and girls who live with cancer. Here are their favorite jokes, as well as those of their camp directors, counselors, family members and friends whose names fill the following pages.

Enjoy the book with the knowledge that children understand the relationship between humor and healing, and when life gets difficult, laughter is the best medicine for all of us.

GARY MERVIS, CHAIRMAN & FOUNDER
CAMP GOOD DAYS & SPECIAL TIMES

20 YEARS
OF CAMP GOOD DAYS & SPECIAL TIMES

Nineteen ninety-nine marks the 20th anniversary of the founding of Camp Good Days and Special Times.

The concept for Camp Good Days began to develop in 1979 when Teddi Mervis was diagnosed with a malignant brain tumor. Her family was devastated. But, through the course of her treatment, her father, Gary, developed a vision which would become her legacy; a camp for children cheated of their childhood by terminal illness and its treatment.

The vision grew and became a summer camp where kids battling childhood cancer could come together to share good days - away from doctors and treatment regimes; a camp filled with warm sunshine and warmer smiles from a dedicated staff and caring volunteers; a camp filled with fun that created lasting memories of special times.

Through the dedication of dozens of staff members, the commitment of hundreds of volunteers, and the generosity of thousands of contributors over the past 20 years, Camp Good Days has grown, expanded and diversified. It has changed from a summer camp for kids with cancer, to a year 'round continuum of programs which ease suffering and provide support for the entire circle of people who are affected by an unforeseen twist of fate - the patient, the parents, the siblings, the grandparents, the friends, the teachers, and the other caregivers and loved ones.

Today, the Camp Good Days' circle of support is reflected through dozens of programs which have become models for agencies working with children who are victims of disease and violence across the United States and around the world.

MANUSCRIPT SPONSORS

The contributions of the following people, corporations and foundations went far beyond funding the manuscript and illustrations for this book. Their commitment to the children, their advice to the editors, and their generosity over the years are gratefully acknowledged and sincerely appreciated.

Richard A. Kaplan, Founder, c.a.r.i.n.g.

Chris McVicker, President, The Flanders Group

Rochester Automobile Dealers' Association
John Lyboldt, Executive Director

Valerie Mannix, President, Mercury Print Productions, Inc.

"Crossroads the Clown"
Illustration by Erin Bennett

Edited by
Michael F. Verno

Illustrated by
Jared J. Camp

DEDICATION

This book is dedicated to Mary Ann
and all caregivers everywhere.
You preserve life's quality.

Copyright (c) 1998 by Michael F. Verno
All rights reserved.
Cataloging-in-Publication Data
Camp Good Days and Special Times, Inc.
Joke Book A to Z
Summary: A collection of childhood jokes submitted by
campers, counselors & friends of children's oncology camps.
ISBN 0-9668130-0-6 4.95
1. Jokes, Juvenile   2. Riddles, Juvenile
I. Verno, Michael F.   II. Camp, Jared J. ill.   III. Title
PN6371.5 1998   818'.5402   00-00000

First Edition 10 9 8 7 6 5 4 3 2 1

FAVORITE JOKES
FROM A TO Z

	page
Apple	8
Bee	10
Cow	12
Dog	14
Elephant	16
Farm	18
Galaxy	20
Halloween	22
Insect	24
Job	26
Kitty	28
Love	30
Medical Doctor	32
Number	34
Ocean	36
People	38
Quackers	40
Rabbit	42
Sports	44
Technology	46
Umbrella	48
Vehicle	50
Woods	52
Xwalk	54
Yum-yum	56
Zoo	58

IS FOR APPLE

Did all of the animals go into Noah's Ark
in pairs?
No. The worms went in apples.

WENDY MERVIS, DIRECTOR, CAMP GOOD DAYS, ROCHESTER, NY

Why did the student give the teacher a tomato
instead of an apple?
He wanted to KETCHUP on his homework.

SHANE, CAMP GOOD DAYS FRIEND, SYRACUSE, NY

Why do apples like to gossip?
They have all the JUICY stuff.

NAOMI, CAMP GOOD DAYS FRIEND, NEW YORK CITY, NY

If you eat 2 apples, is that a pear?

GREG, CAMP GOOD DAYS CAMPER, BUFFALO, NY

How many apples can you put into an empty bag?

One. After that, the bag isn't empty.

CANDACE, CAMP GOOD DAYS CAMPER, TAMPA, FL

Why did the apple stop rolling?

It ran out of JUICE.

ALLEN, CAMP GOOD DAYS FRIEND, ROCHESTER, NY

If an apple and a cabbage ran a race, who would win?

The cabbage because it's a-HEAD.

ERIN, CAMP GOOD DAYS VOLUNTEER, HONEOYE FALLS, NY

Why did the apple fall in love with the banana?

Because the banana had ap-PEEL.

TRACY, CAMP GOOD DAYS FRIEND, JAMESTOWN, NY

What fruit is always in a bad mood?

A CRAB apple.

PAT REISER, DIRECTOR, KAMP K.A.C.E, FARGO, ND

What's worse than finding a worm in your apple?

Finding half a worm.

CHARLES, CAMP GOOD DAYS FRIEND, TORONTO, ONTARIO, CANADA

B
IS FOR BEE

What do bumblebees wear to the beach?
BEE-kinis.

DANA, CAMP RAINBOW CAMPER, AUGUSTA, GA

Which insect gets A's in English?
A SPELLING bee.

AMY, CAMP GOOD DAYS CAMPER, ROCHESTER, NY

What do bees wear to school?
Yellow jackets.

JOHN, CAMP GOOD DAYS CAMPER, BUFFALO, NY

How does a bee part his hair?
With a honey-COMB.

JEREMIAH, CAMP GOOD DAYS FRIEND, ANETA, ND

What do you get if you cross a bee with a telephone?
A BUZZ-y signal.

CAROL HILL, DIRECTOR, CAMP LIVE-A-DREAM, OKLAHOMA CITY, OK

How do bees get to school?
On the school BUZZ.

ALEX, CAMP SMILE-A-MILE CAMPER, BIRMINGHAM, AL

What bee can never be understood?
A MUMBLE-bee.

TINA, CAMP TRILLIUM CAMPER, BLOOMFIELD, ONTARIO, CANADA

Why do bees itch?
Because they have HIVES.

ERIN, CAMP ONE STEP AT A TIME PROJECTS CAMPER,
ELK GROVE VILLAGE, IL

Knock-knock.
Who's there?
Beehive.
Beehive who?
Beehive yourself.

ALLISON, CAMP HAPPY TIMES CAMPER, MAPLEWOOD, NJ

IS FOR COW

What do you call the winner of a beauty pageant for cows?
The DAIRY Queen.

TINA, CAMP RISING SUN CAMPER, WALLINGFORD, CT

What do cows put on their hot dogs?
MOO-stard.

ROY BERNARDI, MAYOR, SYRACUSE, NY

What do you call a cow eating grass?
A lawn MOO-er.

CAROLINE, CAMP GOOD DAYS CAMPER, TAMPA, FL

Why does a cow wear a bell?
Because its HORN doesn't work.
JACK DOYLE, MONROE COUNTY EXECUTIVE, ROCHESTER, NY

What state has the most cows?
MOO-ssouri.
RACHEL, CAMP SUNSHINE CAMPER, ATLANTA, GA

What is the golden rule for cows?
Do unto UDDERS.
SEAN, CAMP FRIENDSHIP CAMPER, SILVER SPRING, MD

What magazine do cattle read?
COWS-MOO-politan.
ELIZABETH, CAMP RAINBOW CAMPER, PHOENIX, AZ

What would you get if you crossed a cow
with a hobo?
A BUM STEER.
MELINDA, THE RAINBOW CONNECTION CAMPER, GALVESTON, TX

What's the most popular TV show for cows?
STEER Trek.
KEVIN, CAMP LIVE-A-DREAM CAMPER, OKLAHOMA CITY, OK

Knock-knock.
Who's there?
Pasture.
Pasture who?
Pasture bedtime.
MATT, CAMP ADVENTURE CAMPER, LONG ISLAND, NY

D
IS FOR DOG

Why is spaghetti a dog's favorite meal?
Because it's PAWS-ta.

BIANCA, CAMP LIVE-A-DREAM, OKLAHOMA CITY, OK

What is a dog's favorite soup?
Chicken POODLE.

AMANDA, CAMP GOOD DAYS FRIEND, ROCHESTER, NY

What kind of dog washes its hair?
A sham-POODLE.

STEFANIE, CAMP GOOD DAYS FRIEND, ROCHESTER, NY

What kind of dog wakes up with its hair
all messed?
Poodles. They get up CURLY in the morning.

JACLYN, CAMP ADVENTURE CAMPER, LONG ISLAND, NY

What do you get when you cross a dog with a chicken?
A chicken that lays POOCHED eggs.

NUTSO, PRESIDENT OF CLOWN ALLEY, BUFFALO, NY

What is it called when 2 dogs kiss?
A POOCH smooch.

JULIE, CAMP GOOD DAYS VOLUNTEER, TAMPA, FL

What dog could jump higher than a house?
Any dog, because a house can't jump.

CHELSEA, CAMP RAINBOW CAMPER, PHOENIX, AZ

What name do you call a dog who surfs the net?
Browser.

JANIS MATTHEWS, DIRECTOR,
THE RAINBOW CONNECTION, GALVESTON, TX

What do you call a flea looking for a ride on a dog?
An ITCH-hiker.

MARK, CAMP RISING SUN CAMPER, WALLINGFORD, CT

Knock-knock.
Who's there?
Flea.
Flea who?
Flea blind mice.

TOM, ONE STEP AT A TIME PROJECTS CAMPER,
ELK GROVE VILLAGE, IL

E
IS FOR ELEPHANT

How do you make an elephant laugh?
Tickle its IVORIES.

ALISSA, CAMP HAPPY TIMES CAMPER, MAPLEWOOD NJ

Why did the elephant cut his vacation short?
He forgot to pack his TRUNK.

SUSANNE, CAMP GOOD DAYS FRIEND, GORLITZ, GERMANY

Why were the elephants thrown out of the swimming pool?
They couldn't keep their TRUNKS up.

JESSICA, CAMP GOOD DAYS VOLUNTEER, ROCHESTER, NY

What did the elephant do when he broke
his toe?
He called a TOE truck.

REBECCA, CAMP GOOD DAYS CAMPER, TAMPA, FL

What do you get when you cross elephants
with fish?
Swimming TRUNKS.

CHRIS, CAMP RAINBOW CAMPER, AUGUSTA, GA

What was the elephant doing on the highway?
About 5 miles an hour.

STEPHEN, CAMP GOOD DAYS VOLUNTEER, ROCHESTER, NY

What do elephants use to wash their tusks?
IVORY soap.

CHLOE, CAMP TRILLIUM CAMPER, BLOOMFIELD, ONTARIO, CANADA

Why are elephant rides cheaper than
pony rides?
Elephants work for PEANUTS.

RACHEL, CAMP LIVE-A-DREAM CAMPER, OKLAHOMA CITY, OK

Why did the elephant buy a bigger car?
He needed more TRUNK space.

FRANKIE, CAMP ADVENTURE CAMPER, LONG ISLAND, NY

F
IS FOR FARM

Why are farms so noisy?
Because all the bulls have HORNS.

JEN, CAMP GOOD DAYS VOLUNTEER, ROCHESTER, NY

What do you call a sleeping bull?
A bull-DOZER.

JOE, CAMP GOOD DAYS CAMPER, ALBANY, NY

On which side does a chicken have the most feathers?
The outside.

LIZ, CAMP GOOD DAYS FRIEND, ROCHESTER, NY

What do pigs put on sores?
OINK-ment.

ERIK, CAMP GOOD DAYS FRIEND, UPPSALA, SWEDEN

How does a pig talk?
SWINE language.

STEVE, CAMP GOOD DAYS VOLUNTEER, ROCHESTER, NY

What do you get when you cross a pig and a dinosaur?
Jurassic PORK.

BARBARA NICHOLS, DIRECTOR, ARIZONA CAMP SUNRISE, PHOENIX, AZ

Why couldn't the pony talk?
Because he was a little HORSE.

GREG, CAMP GOOD DAYS CAMPER, SYRACUSE, NY

Why did they let the turkey join the band?
He had the DRUM-sticks.

SALLY HALE, DIRECTOR, CAMP SUNSHINE, ATLANTA, GA

How should you treat a baby goat?
Like a KID.

PAT WILLIAMS, EXECUTIVE,
ORLANDO MAGIC BASKETBALL, ORLANDO, FL

What does a worm do in a cornfield?
He goes in one EAR and out the other.

RAY, ONE STEP AT A TIME PROJECTS CAMPER, ELK GROVE VILLAGE, IL

Why can't you keep a secret on a farm?
Because the corn has EARS, the potatoes have EYES, and the horses carry TAILS.

SUSAN, CAMP HAPPY TIMES COUNSELOR, MAPLEWOOD, NJ

19

G

IS FOR GALAXY

What do you get if you cross a space ship
with a sausage?
A FLYING SAUSAGE.

JOANN, CAMP GOOD DAYS FRIEND, BUFFALO, NY

How do you get a baby astronaut to go
to sleep?
You ROCK-et.

CURINE, CAMP LIVE-A-DREAM CAMPER, OKLAHOMA CITY, OK

If athletes get athletes foot, what do
astronauts get?
MISSILE toe.

JOEY, CAMP ADVENTURE CAMPER, LONG ISLAND, NY

Why did the silly astronaut attach a rocket to his hamburger?
He liked FAST FOOD.
ANDREW, CAMP FRIENDSHIP CAMPER, SILVER SPRING, MD

Where do astronauts go fishing?
In the galax-SEAS.
KARL, CAMP GOOD DAYS VOLUNTEER, TAMPA, FL

When do astronauts eat?
At LAUNCH time.
JEAN LOCKROW, DIRECTOR, CAMP RAINBOW, PHOENIX, AZ

Where do otters come from?
OTTER space.
BRITTANY, CAMP GOOD DAYS FRIEND, ROCHESTER, NY

What did the Little Dipper say to the Big Dipper?
I want to be a STAR when I grow up.
PATRICK, CAMP ADVENTURE CAMPER, LONG ISLAND, NY

What do guardian angels say when they answer the phone?
HALO.
SAMANTHA, CAMP GOOD DAYS CAMPER, BUFFALO, NY

Knock-knock.
Who's there?
ET.
ET who?
ET your food before it gets cold.
PAUL, CAMP RISING SUN CAMPER, WALLINGFORD, CT

21

H

IS FOR HALLOWEEN

How do witches hold their hair in place?
With SCARE-spray.

ALLISON, CAMP ADVENTURE CAMPER, LONG ISLAND, NY

What do witches play at Halloween parties?
Musical SCARES.

TONY, CAMP SMILE-A-MILE CAMPER, BIRMINGHAM, AL

What do birds say on Halloween?
Twick or TWEET.

MARK, CAMP LIVE-A-DREAM CAMPER, OKLAHOMA CITY, OK

What do you say to a skeleton before he eats?
BONE appetit.

MIKE CATALANA, CHANNEL 13 SPORTS, ROCHESTER, NY

What do you say to a skeleton going on vacation?
BONE voyage.

ANGELA, CAMP GOOD DAYS FRIEND, ROCHESTER, NY

What is Dracula's favorite fruit?
A NECK-tarine.

MARK SYVEROD, WOLFE PUBLICATIONS, VICTOR, NY

Why did the vampire buy a newspaper every day?
To check his HORROR-scope.

LAURA LASKO, DIRECTOR, CAMP RAINBOW, AUGUSTA, GA

What kind of pie do ghosts like to eat?
BOO-berry.

MATTHEW, CAMP RAINBOW CAMPER, PHOENIX, AZ

What's a goblin's favorite kind of music?
Rhythm and BOOS.

JONATHAN, CAMP REACH FOR THE SKY CAMPER, SAN DIEGO, CA

What does a goblin eat for lunch?
A GHOST-ed cheese sandwich.

STEVE, CAMP GOOD DAYS VOLUNTEER, ROCHESTER, NY

Knock-knock.
Who's there?
Boo.
Boo who?
I didn't mean to make you cry.

TRACY, CAMP SMILE-A-MILE CAMPER, BIRMINGHAM, AL

I

IS FOR INSECT

What did the mother lightning bug say to the father lightning bug?
Junior sure is BRIGHT.

GEORGE E. PATAKI, GOVERNOR, NEW YORK STATE

Who takes the photos at an insect's wedding?
A SHUTTER-bug.

CONNOR, CAMP ADVENTURE CAMPER, LONG ISLAND, NY

What do you call a nervous insect?
A JITTER-bug.

MICHELLE, CAMP LIVE-A-DREAM CAMPER, OKLAHOMA CITY, OK

Why was the spider a baseball star?
He was great at catching FLIES.

CHRIS, CAMP GOOD DAYS CAMPER, TAMPA, FL

What is an insect's favorite subject?
MOTH-amatics.

JOHN, CAMP GOOD DAYS FRIEND, ALBANY, NY

How do you start a flea market?
From SCRATCH.

PAT, CAMP GOOD DAYS FRIEND, BLASDELL, NY

How do you start a track meet for fleas?
1, 2, FLEA, go.

KEITH, CAMP HAPPY TIMES COUNSELOR, MAPLEWOOD, NJ

What insects are always polite?
LADY-bugs.

CURTIS, CAMP TRILLIUM CAMPER, BLOOMFIELD, ONTARIO, CANADA

Knock-knock.
Who's there?
Amos.
Amos who?
A mosquito bit me.

SHELBY, CAMP SMILE-A-MILE CAMPER, BIRMINGHAM, AL

J IS FOR JOB

What did the **chef** name his son?
Stew.

JOSIE, CAMP GOOD DAYS COUNSELOR, ROCHESTER, NY

What did the **lawyer** name her daughter?
Sue.

KATIE, CAMP SMILE-A-MILE CAMPER, BIRMINGHAM, AL

If the **police** arrest a mime, do they have to tell him he has the right to remain silent?

ANTHONY MASIELLO, MAYOR, BUFFALO, NY

What kind of uniforms do **paratroopers** wear?
JUMP suits.

JACKIE, CAMP CAN-DO CAMPER, HERSHEY, PA

What do you call a dance held by **butchers**?
A MEAT-ball.

JAY, CAMP GOOD DAYS CAMPER, SYRACUSE, NY

Why did the shy **conductor** stand with his
back to the orchestra?
He couldn't face the music.

DONN, CAMP GOOD DAYS FRIEND, TAMPA, FL

Why did the **burglar** take a shower?
He wanted to make a CLEAN getaway.

BRIAN, CAMP FRIENDSHIP, SILVER SPRING, MD

What kind of stories do **bakers** tell their
children?
BREAD-time stories.

JANIS MATTHEWS, DIRECTOR,
THE RAINBOW CONNECTION, GALVESTON, TX

What did the **TV weatherman** say to the
banker?
I'll take a RAIN check.

JOE RULISON, CAMP GOOD DAYS FRIEND, ROCHESTER, NY

K

IS FOR KITTY

Where does a kitty shop for a new coat?
In a CAT-alog.

PAULINE MCKANNA, DIRECTOR,
CAMP TRILLIUM, BLOOMFIELD, ONTARIO, CANADA

What is a cat's favorite color?
PURR-ple.

ANGIE, CAMP RISING SUN CAMPER, WALLINGFORD, CT

What do cats wear when they go on a date?
PURR-fume.

KATE, CAMP SMILE-A-MILE CAMPER, BIRMINGHAM, AL

What do cats eat for breakfast?
MICE krispies.
CATHY & JOHN, CAMP GOOD DAYS VOLUNTEERS, ROCHESTER, NY

What do cats make for a quick lunch?
Minute MICE.
MATT, CAMP ADVENTURE CAMPER, LONG ISLAND, NY

Where does a cat like to hide?
In a CLAW-set.
KRISTEN, CAMP GOOD DAYS FRIEND, ROCHESTER, NY

What do you call a cat who works at Kinko's?
A COPY cat.
TERRY, CAMP FRIENDSHIP CAMPER, SILVER SPRING, MD

There are 10 copycats in the car. One gets out. How many are left?
None.
KATHERINE, CAMP REACH FOR THE SKY CAMPER, SAN DIEGO, CA

Knock-knock.
Who's there?
Wendy.
Wendy who?
Wendy cats away the mouse will play.
RACHEL, CAMP LIVE-A-DREAM CAMPER, OKLAHOMA CITY, OK

L

IS FOR LOVE

Where do vegetables go to get married?
To the Justice of the PEAS.

CHARLENE, CAMP GOOD DAYS CAMPER, TAMPA, FL

What happened when the boy vampire saw
the girl vampire?
It was love at first BITE.

CHRIS, CAMP FRIENDSHIP CAMPER, SILVER SPRING, MD

What did the canary say to her husband when
he gave her birdseed for her birthday?
CHEEP, CHEEP.

LORI, ONE STEP AT A TIME PROJECTS CAMPER, ELK GROVE VILLAGE, IL

Why did the melons have to have a formal
wedding?
Cant-ELOPE.

CURINE, CAMP LIVE-A-DREAM, OKLAHOMA CITY, OK

What do you call two spiders who were just
married?
Newly WEBS.

JASPER, CAMP ADVENTURE CAMPER, LONG ISLAND, NY

What happened to the two bedbugs who
fell in love?
They got married in the SPRING.

MICHAEL, ARIZONA CAMP SUNRISE, PHOENIX, AZ

Why is an engaged girl like a telephone?
They both have a RING.

MELINDA, THE RAINBOW CONNECTION CAMPER, GALVESTON, TX

What did the boy volcano say to the girl
volcano?
I LAVA you.

DONN ESMONDE, BUFFALO NEWS, BUFFALO, NY

Knock-knock.
Who's there?
Jimmy.
Jimmy who?
Jimmy a little kiss.

ANGELA, CAMP SUNSHINE CAMPER, ATLANTA, GA

M

IS FOR MEDICAL DOCTOR

Why did the cookie go to the doctor?
He was feeling CRUMMY.

PATRICK, CAMP GOOD DAYS CAMPER, SYRACUSE, NY

How long should a doctor practice medicine?
Until he learns to do it right.

ADAM, CAMP FRIENDSHIP SOUTH CAMPER, DUBLIN, OH

Mother: My son just swallowed a roll of film.
Doctor: Let's hope nothing DEVELOPS.

JOE, CAMP HAPPY TIMES COUNSELOR, MAPLEWOOD, NJ

Patient: Doctor!

Doctor: Yes, what is it?

Patient: Will this cream you gave me clear up these red spots on my body?

Doctor: I never make RASH promises.

NATASHA, CAMP LIVE-A-DREAM CAMPER, OKLAHOMA CITY, OK

Cowboy: Doctor, whenever I ride in the rodeo, I don't feel so well. What do you think it could be?

Doctor: BRONC-itis.

JACQUELINE, CAMP CAN-DO CAMPER, HERSHEY, PA

Where do ships go when they get seasick?

To the DOCK-tor.

MARYANNE ESOLEN, DIRECTOR, CAMP ADVENTURE, LONG ISLAND, NY

What did the doctor say to the patient after the operation?

That's enough out of you.

MEGHAN, ARIZONA CAMP SUNRISE CAMPER, PHOENIX, AZ

Can coffee make you feel better when you have the flu?

It made Max-WELL.

NANA BANANA, CAMP GOOD DAYS FRIEND, ROCHESTER, NY

Who comes down the hospital chimney and fills the stockings with bandages?

Santa GAUZE.

CHLOE, CAMP TRILLIUM CAMPER, BLOOMFIELD, ONTARIO, CANADA

IS FOR NUMBER

If I had 6 apples in one hand and 5 in the other, what would I have?
Very big hands.

GEOFFREY, CAMP GOOD DAYS FRIEND, ROCHESTER, NY

If 2 is company and 3 is a crowd, what are 4 and 5?
9.

TOM JOLLS, CHANNEL 7 WEATHER, BUFFALO, NY

If you had 16 cows and 2 goats, what would you have?
Plenty of milk.

THOMAS, ONE STEP AT A TIME PROJECTS CAMPER,
ELK GROVE VILLAGE, IL

What did the 0 say to the 8?
I love your FIGURE.

CHRIS MCVICKER, CAMP GOOD DAYS FRIEND, ROCHESTER, NY

What's a 10-letter word that starts with gas?
Automobile.

ZACHARY, CAMP GOOD DAYS CAMPER, SYRACUSE, NY

What starts with "e" and has only 1 letter in it?
Envelope.

MATT, CAMP FRIENDSHIP CAMPER, SILVER SPRING, MD

What's the longest word in the world?
Smile - there's a MILE from s to e.

ELLEN, CAMP HAPPY TIMES COUNSELOR, MAPLEWOOD, NJ

What is the tallest building in town?
The library. It has hundreds of STORIES.

KARA, ONE STEP AT A TIME PROJECTS CAMPER, ELK GROVE VILLAGE, IL

How are your left hand and 2 + 2 = 5 alike?
Neither is RIGHT.

BARBARA WIGGINS, DIRECTOR,
CAMP REACH FOR THE SKY, SAN DIEGO, CA

What has 3 feet but no toes?
A yardstick.

KATIE, CAMP SMILE-A MILE CAMPER, BIRMINGHAM, AL

O

IS FOR OCEAN

What are the most valuable fish in the ocean?
GOLD-fish.

ASHLEY, CAMP GOOD DAYS FRIEND, ROCHESTER, NY

Why do fish live in salt water?
Because pepper makes them sneeze.

SUSAN, CAMP TRILLIUM CAMPER, BLOOMFIELD, ONTARIO, CANADA

Who rules the ocean underworld?
The COD-father.

MICHAEL, ARIZONA CAMP SUNRISE CAMPER, PHOENIX, AZ

Why can't whales keep a secret?
They're BLUBBER-mouths.

KATHY, CAMP REACH FOR THE SKY CAMPER, SAN DIEGO, CA

What do sharks eat for dinner?
Fish and SHIPS.

BILL PAXON, U.S. REPRESENTATIVE, BUFFALO, NY

Why didn't the shark eat the girl?
Because it was a MAN-eating shark.

TERRY, CAMP FRIENDSHIP CAMPER, SILVER SPRING, MD

Why do fish stay away from computers?
Because they're afraid of getting caught in the INTERNET.

DAVID KOON, NYS ASSEMBLYMAN, ROCHESTER, NY

What did the Cinderella mermaid wear to the ball?
Glass FLIPPERS.

TINA SAUNDER, DIRECTOR, CAMP RISING SUN, WALLINGFORD, CT

Where do fish like to gamble?
At the CLAMS casino.

ANGEL, CAMP RISING SUN, WALLINGFORD, CT

Knock-knock.
Who's there?
Duane.
Duane who?
Duane the water, I'm drowning.

MIRANDA, CAMP GOOD DAYS FRIEND, BUFFALO, NY

P

IS FOR PEOPLE

Why did **Abraham Lincoln** put his bed in the fireplace?
He wanted to sleep like a LOG.

JOHN FARNAN, NYS DEPT. OF SOCIAL SERVICES, ALBANY, NY

Why did they bury **George Washington** standing up?
Because he never LIES.

NICOLE, CAMP GOOD DAYS FRIEND, BUFFALO, NY

What does **Johnny Cash** do when he checks into a motel?
CASH REGISTERS.

T.S., CAMP GOOD DAYS FRIEND, ROCHESTER, NY

What did **Wonder Woman** say to **Spider Man?**
Don't BUG me.

DANA, CAMP RAINBOW CAMPER, AUGUSTA, GA

What did **Cinderella** say when her pictures didn't arrive?
Some day my PRINTS will come.

JASON, CAMP GOOD DAYS CAMPER, SYRACUSE, NY

Why did **Grandma Moses** put wheels on her rocking chair?
Because she wanted to ROCK AND ROLL.

MARY GWENEVIEVE, CAMP GOOD DAYS FRIEND, SAN DIEGO, CA

Who keeps **Santa Claus** company?
CHIMNEY Cricket.

SARAH, CAMP RAINBOW CAMPER, PHOENIX, AZ

Who wears a mask and spreads grass seed wherever he goes?
*The **LAWN** Ranger.*

HEATHER, CAMP ADVENTURE, LONG ISLAND, NY

Knock-knock.
Who's there?
Hello.
Hello who?
Heloise. *Have a hint?*

HELOISE, NATIONALLY SYNDICATED COLUMNIST, "HINTS FROM HELOISE"

Q
IS FOR QUACKERS

What time does a duck get up?
At the QUACK of dawn.

CARLA, CAMP GOOD DAYS CAMPER, TAMPA, FL

Where do ducks go on vacation?
Alba-QUACKY, New Mexico.

RACHEL, CAMP SUNSHINE CAMPER, ATLANTA, GA

A rabbit and a duck went to a show that cost
a dollar. Which one got in?
The duck, because he had a BILL.

JUSTIN, CAMP GOOD DAYS FRIEND, TRENTON, MI

What do you get when you put a duck in a peanut butter jar?
Peanut butter and QUACKERS.

ROOSEVELT, ONE STEP AT A TIME PROJECTS CAMPER, ELK GROVE VILLAGE, IL

How do ducks cure back pain?
With QUACK-upuncture.

ROBERT, CAMP ADVENTURE CAMPER, LONG ISLAND, NY

How do you lift a heavy duck?
With a QUACKER jack.

CHLOE, CAMP TRILLIUM CAMPER, BLOOMFIELD, ONTARIO, CANADA

How can you tell the price of a duck?
Check the BILL.

MICHAEL, KAMP K.A.C.E. CAMPER, FARGO, ND

What do you get when you cross a cow with a duck?
Milk and QUACKERS.

CAROLINE, CAMP GOOD DAYS CAMPER, TAMPA, FL

What kind of doctor treats ducks?
A QUACK.

PAT DOLL, DIRECTOR, CAMP CAN-DO, HERSHEY, PA

How do you get down from a giraffe?
You don't. You get DOWN from a duck.

JENNY, CAMP GOOD DAYS VOLUNTEER, ROCHESTER, NY

R

IS FOR RABBIT

Where does a rabbit go when its coat needs grooming?
To the HARE dresser.

STEPHANIE, CAMP GOOD DAYS FRIEND, LANCASTER, PA

How do rabbits keep cool in summer?
Central HARE conditioning.

KAREN, ONE STEP AT A TIME PROJECTS CAMPER,
ELK GROVE VILLAGE, IL

What do you get when you cross a rabbit with a spider?
A HARE-net.

SUSAN, CAMP TRILLIUM CAMPER, BLOOMFIELD, ONTARIO, CANADA

What is a rabbit's favorite song?
HOP-py Birthday.

ALEXIS, CAMP GOOD DAYS FRIEND, ROCHESTER, NY

What would you call a rabbit that's stuck in the mud?
Un-HOP-py.

BRYAN, CAMP ADVENTURE CAMPER, LONG ISLAND, NY

What did the rabbits say when the farmer caught them in the garden?
LETTUCE alone.

GARY, KAMP K.A.C.E. CAMPER, FARGO, ND

Why are rabbits good mathematicians?
They know how to MULTIPLY.

JAMES, CAMP HAPPY TIMES CAMPER, MAPLEWOOD, NJ

Where do rabbits go when they get married?
On their BUNNY-moon.

PATRICIA, THE RAINBOW CONNECTION CAMPER, GALVESTON, TX

How do rabbits go on vacation?
Via TransWorld HARE-lines.

BEVERLY GOUGH, DIRECTOR, CAMP FRIENDSHIP, SILVER SPRING, MD

What city in the State of New York has the most rabbits?
Albany (All BUNNY).

JANET, CAMP GOOD DAYS FRIEND, ALBANY, NY

S

IS FOR SPORTS

Why did the baseball player bring a rope to the ballpark?
He wanted to TIE UP the game.

TIM, CAMP GOOD DAYS CAMPER, SYRACUSE, NY

Why should you always take a baseball player when you go camping?
To PITCH the tent.

MARV FOLEY, MANAGER, ROCHESTER RED WINGS, ROCHESTER, NY

Are baseball umpires good eaters?
Absolutely. They always clean their PLATES.

NICHOLAS J. PIRRO, ONONDAGA COUNTY EXECUTIVE, SYRACUSE, NY

What happened to the baseball player who was late for dinner?

His wife threw him out at HOME.

WILLIAM JOHNSON, JR., MAYOR, ROCHESTER, NY

What professional athletes are the sloppiest eaters?

Basketball players. They DRIBBLE all over.

JOHN GABRIEL, GENERAL MANAGER, ORLANDO MAGIC, ORLANDO, FL

Why should a football player always carry a pencil?

In case he needs an extra POINT.

LAURA, CAMP GOOD DAYS FRIEND, TAMPA, FL

Where do hockey players stay when they visit New York City?

The Empire SKATE building.

ADAM, CAMP FRIENDSHIP SOUTH CAMPER, DUBLIN, OH

What illness do hockey players fear most?

Chicken PUCKS.

RICH FUNKE, WHEC-TV SPORTS, ROCHESTER, NY

What did the dentist say to the golfer?

You have a HOLE IN ONE and a CHIP in another.

SAL DEBIASE, CAMP GOOD DAYS FRIEND, ROCHESTER, NY

T

IS FOR TECHNOLOGY

What do overworked computer programmers do?
They go home and CRASH.

JORDAN, CAMP GOOD DAYS CAMPER, SYRACUSE, NY

When is it time to take a computer to the doctor?
When it loses its MEMORY.

MELINDA, THE RAINBOW CONNECTION CAMPER, GALVESTON, TX

What happened to the computer that went out in a blizzard?
It got frost-BYTE.

STANLEY, CAMP ADVENTURE CAMPER, LONG ISLAND, NY

Why isn't Dottie ever upset in a chat room?
Because she's DOT CALM.
LAUREN, CAMP CAN-DO CAMPER, HERSHEY, PA

Where do you find the world's biggest spider?
On the worldwide WEB.
CALI, CAMP GOOD DAYS FRIEND, ROCHESTER, NY

How does a computer buff order food in a restaurant?
From a PULL-DOWN MENU.
LYNN THOMPSON, DIRECTOR, CAMP SMILE-A-MILE, BIRMINGHAM, AL

How do you communicate with a fish?
You get him ONLINE.
MIKEY, CAMP GOOD DAYS VOLUNTEER, ROCHESTER, NY

How does a skunk make phone calls?
With a SMELL-ular phone.
KYLE, ARIZONA CAMP SUNRISE CAMPER, PHOENIX, AZ

What do VCR tapes do on vacation?
They UNWIND.
COREY, CAMP SMILE-A-MILE CAMPER, BIRMINGHAM, AL

Knock-knock.
Who's there?
Icon.
Icon who?
Icon get online faster than you.
JAIMIE, CAMP GOOD DAYS VOLUNTEER, ROCHESTER, NY

47

U

IS FOR UMBRELLA

When does it rain money?
When there's CHANGE in the weather.

MARY, CAMP SUNSHINE CAMPER, ATLANTA, GA

Why do you have to be careful when it's raining cats and dogs?
You might step in a POODLE.

JOSH, CAMP SUNSHINE CAMPER, ATLANTA, GA

What kind of sheets do ghosts wear during freezing rain storms?
SHEETS of ice.

MAC, CAMP LIVE-A-DREAM CAMPER, OKLAHOMA CITY, OK

Why did the mother put her little boy under a beach umbrella?
She wanted to prevent SON burn.

MILLIE FINKEL, DIRECTOR, CAMP HAPPY TIMES, MAPLEWOOD, NJ

What can go up the chimney down, but cannot go down the chimney up?
An umbrella.

KALI, CAMP GOOD DAYS FRIEND, ROCHESTER, NY

If a farmer raises corn when the sun shines, what does he raise when it rains?
His umbrella.

JENNIFER, KAMP K.A.C.E. CAMPER, FARGO, ND

What's the difference between rain and snow?
Rain comes in SHEETS and snow in BLANKETS.

DWIGHT, CAMP ADVENTURE CAMPER, LONG ISLAND, NY

Why did the rabbit use an umbrella?
He didn't want his HARE to get wet.

VINNY, CAMP ADVENTURE CAMPER, LONG ISLAND, NY

Knock-knock.
Who's there?
Wayne.
Wayne who?
Wayne drops keep falling on my head.

BARBARA, CAMP GOOD DAYS FRIEND, ROCHESTER, NY

IS FOR VEHICLE

What do you call a vehicle that seats 2 whales in front and 2 whales in back?
A 4-WHALE drive.

TINA SAUNDER, DIRECTOR, CAMP RISING SUN, WALLINGFORD, CT

Where do pigs park their cars?
In PORK-ing lots.

FRANKIE, CAMP SMILE-A-MILE CAMPER, BIRMINGHAM, AL

What happens to a frog's car when the parking meter expires?
It gets TOAD away.

LACEY, CAMP LIVE-A-DREAM CAMPER, OKLAHOMA CITY, OK

What was the turtle doing on the freeway?
About 150 inches an hour.

ROSALINE, CAMP ADVENTURE CAMPER, LONG ISLAND, NY

What do clowns do when they get into a vehicle?
They CHUCKLE up.

JOYCE, CAMP GOOD DAYS FRIEND, ROCHESTER, NY

What does a mother ghost say to her children when they get into the car?
Fasten your SHEET belts.

ROSE, CAMP GOOD DAYS FRIEND, TRENTON, MI

What did the little tire want to be when he grew up?
A big WHEEL.

KATHERINE, CAMP REACH FOR THE SKY CAMPER, SAN DIEGO, CA

Why did the man repair the horn on his car?
It didn't give a TOOT.

ANDY, CAMP RAINBOW CAMPER, PHOENIX, AZ

Why was the auto mechanic fired?
He took too many BRAKES.

JON, CAMP SMILE-A-MILE CAMPER, BIRMINGHAM, AL

What would you get if you crossed a kangaroo with an auto mechanic?
JUMPER cables.

LON, CAMP ADVENTURE CAMPER, LONG ISLAND, NY

W

IS FOR WOODS

How do you stop a skunk from smelling?
Put a clothes pin on his nose.

J.P., CAMP GOOD DAYS FRIEND, ROCHESTER, NY

Why did the skunk go into the restaurant?
So he could place his ODOR.

MISSY, CAMP GOOD DAYS CAMPER, BUFFALO, NY

What do frogs wear in the summer?
Open TOAD shoes.

DOROTHY, CAMP GOOD DAYS FRIEND, ROCHESTER, NY

What do frogs drink?
CROAK-a-cola.

BO, CAMP GOOD DAYS CAMPER, TAMPA, FL

What's a frogs favorite year?
LEAP year.
KEVIN E. WALSH, ONONDAGA COUNTY SHERIFF, SYRACUSE, NY

What do snakes do after they have a fight?
They HISS and make up.
DIANE MESH, PROGRAM DIRECTOR,
ONE STEP AT A TIME PROJECTS, ELK GROVE VILLAGE, IL

What kind of birds stick together?
Vel-CROWS.
TIM, CAMP GOOD DAYS CAMPER, SYRACUSE, NY

Why do birds fly south?
Because it's too far to walk.
NANCY PALUMBO, NYS OFFICE OF PARKS, ALBANY, NY

Why do male deer smile so much?
To show off their BUCK teeth.
ROBBY, ONE STEP AT A TIME PROJECTS CAMPER,
ELK GROVE VILLAGE, IL

What do you call Smokey and 5 of his relatives?
A 6-pack of BEAR.
NICK, CAMP GOOD DAYS FRIEND, DETROIT, MI

What animal do you look like in the shower?
A little BEAR.
BUDDY, CAMP ADVENTURE CAMPER, LONG ISLAND, NY

X

IS FOR CROSS-WALK

Why didn't the rooster cross the road?
Because he was CHICKEN.

ROBERTA MCLURE, DIRECTOR, BIG SKY KIDS, BILLINGS, MT

Why did the turtle cross the road?
To get to the SHELL station.

CHAD BRATZKE, NEW YORK GIANTS FOOTBALL, NEW YORK, NY

Why did the cow cross the road?
To get to the UDDER side.

ALLISON, CAMP HAPPY TIMES FRIEND, MAPLEWOOD, NJ

Why did the naughty goose cross the road to the playground?
To join in the FOWL play.

CATHY, CAMP GOOD DAYS VOLUNTEER
COORDINATOR, ROCHESTER, NY

Why did the cowboy cross the road?
Just to HORSE around.

JOSH, CAMP GOOD DAYS CAMPER, ROCHESTER, NY

Why did the weasel cross the road twice?
Because she was a DOUBLE-CROSSER.

MARC, KAMP K.A.C.E. CAMPER, FARGO, ND

Why did the human cannon ball cross the road?
He was FIRED.

LAURA, CAMP GOOD DAYS CAMPER, ROCHESTER, NY

How did the egg cross the road?
It SCRAMBLED across.

SALLY HALE, DIRECTOR, CAMP SUNSHINE, ATLANTA, GA

Why didn't the orange make it across the road?
Because it didn't have enough JUICE.

RAY, ONE STEP AT A TIME PROJECTS CAMPER, ELK GROVE VILLAGE, IL

IS FOR YUM-YUM

What did the banana say after it got a sunburn?
I hope I don't PEEL.

JESSICA, CAMP GOOD DAYS CAMPER, ROCHESTER, NY

What did one hot dog say to the other?
Hi, FRANK.

BENJAMIN, CAMP GOOD DAYS FRIEND, ROCHESTER, NY

How do you introduce a hamburger?
MEAT patty.

GINNY RYAN, CHANNEL 13 NEWS, ROCHESTER, NY

What fruits are most often mentioned in history?
DATES.

MARY, CAMP GOOD DAYS FRIEND, BUFFALO, NY

What do you get if you cross a cookie with a burglar?
A CROOK-ie.

JOAN, CAMP GOOD DAYS FRIEND, BUFFALO, NY

Have you heard the joke about the peach?
It was PIT-iful.

STEPHANIE, CAMP GOOD DAYS CAMPER, TAMPA, FL

Who is the father of all corn?
POP-corn.

HEATHER, CAMP ADVENTURE CAMPER, LONG ISLAND, NY

What do apes serve for dessert?
Chocolate CHIMP cookies.

MARY ELLEN, CAMP GOOD DAYS FRIEND, ROCHESTER, NY

Why did the ice cream cone take Karate lessons?
He was tired of getting LICKED.

DANIELLE, CAMP GOOD DAYS FRIEND, BOSTON, MA

Knock-knock.
Who's there?
Pizza.
Pizza who?
Pizza nice guy when you get to know him.

JOHN, CAMP REACH FOR THE SKY CAMPER, SAN DIEGO, CA

Z

IS FOR ZOO

What kind of TV do zebras like best?
Black and white.

JASON, CAMP GOOD DAYS CAMPER, SYRACUSE, NY

How do you make a zebra float?
*Put two scoops of ice cream, some milk and
soda water in a glass. Add one zebra.*

KORDI, CAMP GOOD DAYS FRIEND, TRENTON, MI

How do they repair plumbing at the zoo?
With a MONKEY wrench.

JACK, CAMP CAN-DO CAMPER, HERSHEY, PA

Why is the zoo lit up all night?
Because of all the MONKEY shines.

JUSTIN, CAMP RAINBOW CAMPER, PHOENIX, AZ

What kind of key is too big for your pocket?
A mon-KEY.

MELISSA, CAMP GOOD DAYS CAMPER, BUFFALO, NY

Why did the tiger eat the tight rope walker?
He wanted a WELL-BALANCED meal.

JEREMY, CAMP GOOD DAYS FRIEND, ROCHESTER, NY

What time is it when a rhino sits on your chair?
Time to get a new chair.

ADAM, CAMP FRIENDSHIP SOUTH CAMPER, DUBLIN, OH

What happens when giraffes moving west get blocked by giraffes moving east?
A GIRAFFIC jam.

JOHN, CAMP REACH FOR THE SKY CAMPER, SAN DIEGO, CA

Knock-knock.
Who's there?
Zoo.
Zoo who?
Zoo long for now.

JOEY, CAMP SMILE-A-MILE, BIRMINGHAM, AL

ACKNOWLEDGEMENTS

We gratefully acknowledge the talents of the people who created this book and the special friends who managed the project.

Creative & Editorial
Barbara Schreier, Creative Coordinator
Jared Camp, Illustrations & Cover Design
C. Jean Penner, Book Layout & Electronic Art
Erin Bennett, Submissions Coordinator & Spot Illustrations
Joe Manuse, Manuse Design, Art Director
Jean Verno, Research Consultant

Management & Marketing
Chris McVicker, Project Originator
Susan DeBlase, Management Consultant
Cathy Linfoot, Camp Correspondent
Karen Hoerner, Distribution Advisor
Kevin Meath, Media Consultant

Printing & Production
Joe Aquilino, Mercury Print Productions, Inc.
Kent Campbell, Campbell Photos, Inc., Photographer

Distribution Sponsors
Gratitude is also extended to Tops Friendly Markets and Vix Deep Discount for serving as our distribution sponsors. Thank you.

SINCERE APPRECIATION

This book was created through the generous contribution of time and submission of jokes from the campers, counselors, volunteers, staff, directors and friends of Camp Good Days and Special Times and the following children's oncology camps in the United States and Canada. Sincere appreciation to all of you.

Alabama	Camp Smile-A-Mile
Arizona	Arizona Camp Sunrise
Arizona	Camp Rainbow
California	Camp Reach for the Sky
Connecticut	Camp Rising Sun
Georgia	Camp Rainbow
Georgia	Camp Sunshine
Illinois	One Step at a Time Projects
Maryland	Camp Friendship
Montana	Big Sky Kids
North Dakota	Kamp K.A.C.E.
New Jersey	Camp Happy Times
New York	Camp Adventure
Ohio	Camp Friendship
Oklahoma	Camp Live-A-Dream
Ontario, Canada	Camp Trillium
Pennsylvania	Camp Can-Do
Texas	The Rainbow Connection

ORDER ADDITIONAL COPIES

Order additional copies of the Camp Good Days Joke Book A to Z for yourself or as a gift. When you do, you bring the joy of humor to those close to you and help improve the quality of life for children touched by cancer.

So, enjoy a good laugh and support a good cause. Order additional copies as a gift for your family, friends, business clients and customers.

INDIVIDUAL AND BUSINESS ORDERS CALL:

CAMP GOOD DAYS
& SPECIAL TIMES
1332 PITTSFORD-MENDON RD.
MENDON, NY 14506

800-785-2135

"Crossroads the Clown"
Illustration by Erin Bennett

"Crossroads the Clown"
is the official mascot of
Camp Good Days & Special Times,
Rochester, NY
Illustration by Erin Bennett